JETLINER
GENERATION

JETLINER GENERATION

Classic Early Airliners, 1958–1979

MARTIN W. BOWMAN

Airlife
England

Copyright © 2001 Martin W. Bowman

First published in the UK in 2001
by Airlife Publishing Ltd

British Library Cataloguing-in-Publication Data
   A catalogue record for this book
   is available from the British Library

ISBN 1 84037 1641

Typeset by Rowland Phototypesetting Ltd, Bury St Edmunds,
Suffolk.
Printed in China.

Airlife Publishing Ltd

101 Longden Road, Shrewsbury, SY3 9EB, England
E-mail: airlife@airlifebooks.com
Website: www.airlifebooks.com

OPPOSITE:
An American in Paris. On 13 October
1955 Pan American agreed to purchase
six Boeing 707-121s. On 26 October
1958, it was the first airline to place
the aircraft in service, using it on its
New York–Paris route. Boeing 707-121
N707PA *Clipper Maria* first flew on 21
March 1958 and it was delivered to the
airline on 19 December. In December
1964 N707PA was converted to 707-
121B configuration. N707PA was not
withdrawn from service until
November 1980. It was finally broken
up in May 1988.
(*Boeing*)

Author's note

Jetliner Generation is the second of three Airlife airliner titles covering European, the US, and Russian commercial jets. *Piston-powered Propliners* covered the piston-engined airliners and *Timeless Turboprops* the turbine-powered aircraft of the same period. *Wide Bodies* will cover the American 'jumbos' and the wide-bodied aircraft from Europe and Russia. The majority of data and individual aircraft histories for the aircraft in all three titles has been obtained from those invaluable tomes: *Jet Airliner Production List*, *Turbo Prop Airliner Production List* and *Piston Engine Airliner Production List*, all produced by Messrs John Roach and Tony Eastwood. Copies are available from The Aviation Hobby Shop, 4 Horton Parade, Horton Road, West Drayton, Middlesex, UB7 8EA. Details of aircraft accidents have mostly been taken from *Airlife's Register of Aircraft Accidents*, compiled by Antonio Bordoni.

Acknowledgements

Once again, I must make special mention of the City of Norwich Aviation Museum (CONAM) and Graham M. Simons and his wife Anne, both of GMS Enterprises, who provided the foundation for this book with a wealth of transparencies. I am also very grateful to all of the following people, each of whom loaned photos and slides, as well as their time and expertise: Mike Bailey; Darryl Cott; Jerry Cullum; Graham Dinsdale of Ian Allan Travel; Tony and Janet Eastwood; Ron Green; David Grimer; Tony Hudson; Derek N. James; Ben Jones; Phil Kemp; Stan Lee; Barry Reeve; Jerry Scutts, Kelvin Sloper; Walt Truax; and United Airlines.

Martin W. Bowman
Norwich

In June 1955 Douglas belatedly tried to compete with Boeing's 707, announcing that it was entering the long-range jet transport field with the not dissimilar DC-8. However, Douglas was too late to mount a serious challenge. By the end of 1961, while only 176 DC-8s had been sold, Boeing had 320 orders for 707s and 720s. DC-8-11 N8018D, which first flew on 29 December 1958, is pictured in May 1959 at Baltimore's Friendship Airport, Maryland, where United Airlines, the first and largest purchaser of the DC-8, handled ground operations. Friendship was the jet airport for the Washington area at this time as National could not handle jet aircraft and Dulles had not been built. General Curtis E. LeMay, Chief of Staff, USAF, was taken for a flight in May 1959. In August 1960 N8018D was converted to DC-8-21 configuration and was delivered to United as N8001U, being named *Mainliner Warren Burke* on 1 November 1960. Boeing bought the aircraft on 23 January 1978 and stored it at Kingman, Arizona.
(*Walt Truax*)

LEFT AND BELOW:
Aeroflot Tupolev Tu-104A was the first commercial Soviet aircraft to land in the US in spring 1958, carrying the Soviet Ambassador, Mr Mikoyan, his wife and staff. Upon landing it blew a tyre and the crew would not let the fixed-base operator assist in any way. The crew carried everything needed in the belly pits for changing the tyre. Deliveries of production Tu-104s to Aeroflot began in May 1956 and the aircraft entered service with the airline on 15 September that year. The Tu-104A had increased seating capacity, for up to seventy passengers, and went into service with Aeroflot in 1958.
(*Walt Truax*)

Douglas DC-8-11 N8028D first flew on 22 December 1958 and it was converted to a DC-8-12 in March 1961. On 11 May 1961 the aircraft was delivered to United Airlines as N8002U. In April 1965 it was converted again, this time to DC-8-21. N8002U was withdrawn from use early in 1978 and after storage at Detroit–Willow Run, Illinois, it was finally broken up in May 1983.

8   (*via GMS*)

Between 1957 and 1992 Boeing delivered 855 Model 707s in all three versions: 707-120, -320 and -420 intercontinental airliners. No fewer than 725 of these aircraft, delivered between 1957 and 1978, were for commercial use. Boeing 707-328 F-BHSB was the eighty-first 707 off the production lines and first flew on 14 November 1959. It was delivered to Air France on 12 December 1959 and was named *Château de Chambord*. Sierra Bravo was leased to Cameroon Airlines in December 1971 and then returned to Air France in June 1974. In June 1975 F-BHSB was withdrawn from service and stored at Paris–Orly, where it was broken up in 1977.
(*via GMS*)

LEFT:
Boeing 707-437 N5089K first flew on 14 January 1960 and was accepted by Air India as VT-DJI *Nandi Devi* on 18 February that year. Juliet India was destroyed after overrunning the runway at Bombay, India, on 23 January 1971.
(*via GMS*)

ABOVE:
Boeing 707-441 PP-VJA (N5090K) of VARIG. This aircraft first flew on 2 April 1960 and was accepted by the Brazilian airline on 7 June. RDC Marine bought PP-VJA on 10 April 1979 and the aircraft was stored at Houston, Texas, until it was acquired by Business Cash Flow Aviation in July 1989. The following July it was broken up for spares.
(*via GMS*)

BELOW:
Douglas DC-8-41 CF-TJB (N6578C) was accepted by Trans Canada Airlines as Fleet No. 802 on 25 May 1960. Juliet Bravo joined Air Canada on 1 June 1964 and was then bought by Transvalair in June 1977. In June 1977 CF-TJB was withdrawn from service and stored at Sion, Switzerland. Juliet Bravo was broken up in December that year.
(*via GMS*)

Douglas DC-8-42 I-DIWA *Amerigo Vespucci* was accepted by Alitalia on 28 April 1960. Whiskey Alpha was bought by International Air Leases Inc. on 10 October 1977, and in October 1978 it was converted to DC-8-43F configuration. In November 1978 it was leased to Aeronaves del Peru as OB-R1143 *San Martin de Porres*. On 1 August 1980 OB-R1143 crashed at Cerro Lilio, twenty-four kilometres from Mexico City.
(via GMS)

Douglas DC-8-21 (N8611) XA-XAX *20 de Noviembre* of Aeronaves de Mexico, which leased the aircraft from original customer Eastern Airlines on 1 November 1960. On 19 January 1961 Alpha X-ray was damaged beyond repair after an aborted take-off from Idlewild Airport, New York.

(*Douglas via GMS*)

LEFT:
Boeing 707-344 ZS-CKC *Johannesburg* first flew on 25 May 1960 and it was delivered to South African Airways (SAA) on 1 July 1960. Kilo Charlie was purchased by British Midland Airways on 27 July 1977, and it was later operated under lease by other airlines. Finally, in September 1984 it was bought by Columbia Picture Industries and put into storage.
(*via GMS*)

BELOW:
Douglas DC-8-32 F-BJLB was accepted by UTA (Union de Transports Aériens) on 5 August 1960. Lima Bravo was converted to DC-8-33 configuration in May 1965. On 15 February 1979, Air Afrique bought this aircraft, now TU-TCP, and on 6 May 1985 it was acquired by Farner Air Service AG. That same year Charlie Papa was bought by Zurich Airport Authority, and used for training.
(*via GMS*)

Boeing 707-430 D-ABOF *Munchen* first flew on 9 September 1960. One of five 707-430s delivered to Lufthansa, it was accepted on 1 October 1960. D-ABOF was used extensively by DETA Mozambique Airlines, SABENA, Geminair and Egyptair. Oscar Foxtrot's last owner was Liberian Overseas Airways, which bought the aircraft, now registered EL-AJC, in July 1983. It was withdrawn from service and stored at Bournemouth–Hurn Airport in July 1983 and was broken up that August. (*via GMS*)

The Boeing 720 was a lighter-weight, shorter-bodied version of the basic 707, designed specifically for operation on shorter air routes. Boeing 720-048 EI-ALA *St Patrick* first flew on 14 October 1960 and it was accepted by Irish International Airlines (IIA) on 25 October. IIA retired the aircraft on 27 April 1969, and it was used by Trans Polar as LN-TUU *Roald Amundsen* in 1970 before being repossessed by Aer Lingus as *St Pappin* in 1971. In its later years, the aircraft was operated by Club International Inc., as N734T, and Pioneer International, as *City of Niagara Falls*, before being leased. It was finally broken up in 1983. (*via GMS*)

The prototype Convair 880 (N801TW) was photographed at Denver, Colorado, September 1960. The Model 22, or Convair Jet 880 – a figure derived from the cruising speed when converted to feet per second – first flew on 27 January 1959. One potentially disastrous incident during high-speed flutter tests, when most of the rudder was lost, was averted and a safe landing was made at Edwards AFB, California. N8801E, the fourth production Convair 880-22-2, was the first Model 22 to have a passenger interior and to be completed to delivery standards. It was accepted by Delta Air Lines on 10 February 1960. It was flown from San Diego to Miami in three hours and thirty-one minutes, a new transcontinental speed record. Delta put the Convair 880 into service on 15 May, flying between New York and Houston, Texas. In total, Delta Air Lines received seventeen Convair 880s. N801TW, meanwhile, was reregistered N8489H in 1961 and it was delivered to Trans World Airlines (TWA) as N871TW on 20 October 1964. TWA ultimately received twenty-seven Convair 880s, although four of the original order were immediately leased to Northeast Airlines, which went on to operate ten aircraft. N871TW was withdrawn from airline service in 1983.

(*Walt Truax*)

15

Eau de Cologne. Boeing 720-030B D-ABOH *Koln* first flew on 14 February 1961 and was accepted by Lufthansa on 8 March 1961. Pan American bought Oscar Hotel on 12 March 1964, naming it *Clipper Bonita*. On 20 July 1973 the aircraft, now HK-677, was sold to AVIANCA (Aerovias Nacionales de Columbia), and in 1973 it was named *Liborio Mejia*. The aircraft was broken up in 1981. (*via GMS*)

Boeing 720-027 N7077 first flew on 16 March 1961 and it was accepted by Braniff on 22 March 1966. N7077 was subsequently bought by American Aviation Services Inc., on 21 August 1971, and it was leased to Aeromerica in April 1975, before being withdrawn from service. N7077 was stored at Boeing Field in January 1981 and then broken up. (*via GMS*)

Boeing 707-458 4X-ATA *Shehecheyanu* first flew on 14 April 1961 and was accepted by El Al eight days later. Tango Alpha was finally withdrawn from service and broken up in July 1984.

(*via GMS*)

Spanish lady. Douglas DC-8-52 EC-ARB *El Greco* was delivered to Iberia on 27 May 1961. Romeo Bravo was widely used during its long flying career, and was finally withdrawn from service in 1992. It was used for spares by American International Airways.
(*via GMS*)

ABOVE:
Convair (Model 30) 990-30-6 HB-ICC *St Gallen*, photographed in March 1970, was accepted by Swissair on 25 January 1962. Swissair and SAS (Scandinavian Airlines System) had placed a joint order for the Model 31 in 1958 but in 1959 the order was changed to the Model 30. (The Model 31 was not built.) Swissair used the name Coronado for its 990 fleet and it was also adopted by other carriers. The Convair 990 had additional fuel capacity for intercontinental routes and much higher operating weights. Swissair started services with the Coronado on Far East routes on 9 March 1962. *St Gallen* was donated to the Lucerne Traffic Museum on 20 March 1975.
(*Graham Simons*)

Convair 990-30A-5 N5619 was accepted by American Airlines on 23 June 1962. On 19 October 1968, the aircraft, now registered OD-AEW, was acquired by Lebanese International Airways. Echo Whiskey was destroyed in the Israeli commando attack on Beirut on 28 December 1968.
(*via GMS*)

De Havilland Comet 4C G-ASDZ first flew on 5 November 1962 and it was initially to have been used by Mexicana as XA-NAD. Instead, Delta Zulu (and Comet 4C ST-AAX, the final Hatfield-built Comet, which had also been destined for Mexicana), was bought by Sudan Airways. The airline took delivery of ST-AAW on 13 November 1962. ST-AAW was withdrawn from service in October 1973 and stored at Khartoum. On 2 June 1975 Dan Air bought the airliner, now registered G-ASDZ. Delta Zulu was withdrawn from service in October 1975 and was broken up at Lasham, Hampshire.

(*Darryl Cott*)

Hawker Siddeley HS 121 Trident G-ARPC first flew on 25 August 1962 and it was accepted by British European Airways on 9 September 1964. Papa Charlie was damaged beyond economical repair by a cabin fire while parked at London–Heathrow on 28 December 1975.
(*via GMS*)

Douglas DC-8-53 JA8009 Shima was accepted by Japan Asia Airlines on 16 July 1963. The aircraft was subsequently bought by Minerve on 5 March 1982 and reregistered F-GDPM. Papa Mike was withdrawn from service in October 1989 and put into storage at Opa Locka, Florida.
(*via GMS*)

RIGHT:
Regal lady. Douglas DC-8-43 CF-CPJ *Empress of Toronto* was delivered to Canadian Pacific Airlines on 3 May 1963 as '605'. In April 1969 605 was renamed *Empress of Mexico City*. Papa Juliet was bought by ARCA Columbia on 9 December 1981, before being withdrawn from service and put into storage in Miami, Florida.
(*via GMS*)

BELOW:
BAC One-Eleven 201AC G-ASJA, the second One-Eleven to fly, on 19 December 1963. Juliet Alpha was accepted by BUA on 11 October 1965.
(*via Derek James*)

Double echo. Sud-Aviation S.E.210-VIN Caravelle (F-WJAL) first flew on 19 April 1963 and it was delivered to Middle East Airlines as OD-AEE on 26 April 1964. It was one of several aircraft, including three of MEA's four Comet 4Cs, all ordered in January 1960, which were destroyed in the Israeli commando raid on Beirut, Lebanon, on 28 December 1968. Vickers Viscount V.754D 00-ACW (behind) was bought by Aloha Airlines on 30 May 1965. It was damaged beyond repair after a ground collision with a DC-9 at Honolulu, Hawaii, on 27 June 1969.

(*via GMS*)

ABOVE:
First registered G-ASUF, on 30 June 1964, BAC One-Eleven 203AE N1541 made its maiden flight on 9 June 1964, and Braniff Airways accepted the aircraft on 6 July 1965. It was last operated by Amway Corporation Ltd, 1975–6. On 26 August 1991 N1541 was bought by Nationwide Advertising Inc.

(*via GMS*)

BELOW:
Boeing planned to build 250 Model 727 aircraft, but they proved so popular that a total of 1,832 were produced at the Renton plant. Boeing 727-78 9Y-TCO made its maiden flight on 10 December 1964 and was delivered to its first customer, British West Indian Airways, on 21 December. On 8 June 1971 Charlie Oscar was bought by Braniff Airways, which in August 1976 sold it to Transbrasil as PT-TYR. Evergreen International Airlines bought Yankee Romeo on 15 April 1984. PT-TYR was converted to Boeing 727-78F configuration in December 1984.

(*GMS*)

BAC One-Eleven 203AE N1543 first flew on 10 February 1965 and it was accepted by Braniff Airways on 11 March 1965. The aircraft was finally withdrawn from service in 1990 and stored at Orlando, Florida.
(*via GMS*)

Boeing 727-46 JA8307 *Tone* first flew
on 9 July 1965, and it was accepted by
Japan Airlines (JAL) six days later.
Tone was later operated by Korean
Airlines, AVIANCA and SAM
Colombia.
(*via GMS*)

Boeing 720-059B HK-726 *Narino* first flew on 24 March 1965 and was delivered to AVIANCA on 8 April 1965. *Narino* later served with several other airlines, including Monarch Aviation, Jet Star Inc., and Silver Wings, before it was bought by Boeing on 2 October 1984. Boeing put the aircraft to use in the KC-135E military programme. HK-726 was finally broken up in March 1991. (*GMS*)

Boeing 727-22 N7033U first flew on 29 April 1965 and it was accepted by United Airlines on 12 May. The aircraft was later operated by Allegheny Airlines, USAir and AVENSA, before being bought by TAESA on 2 July 1991.

(*GMS*)

Magical girl. Boeing 727-35 N4618 first flew on 10 September 1965 and on 24 September it was accepted by National Airlines. In 1971 National Airlines christened the aircraft *Rita*, Number 18 in the fleet. Pan American took over National, and on 7 January 1980, N4618 became *Clipper Wizard*. Intercredit Corporation bought the aircraft in September 1984 and in the mid-to-late 1980s, N4618 was leased to Flight International Airlines and AVIANCA.

(*GMS*)

Boeing 707-385C N68657 first flew on 13 September 1965, and it was bought by LAN Chile, as CC-CEB, on 20 December 1969. In 1981 the aircraft was named *Lago Ranco*. Ten years later *Lago Ranco* was bought by the Chilean Air Force.

(*Jerry C. Scutts*)

Hawker Siddeley Trident 1E-ATNA first flew on 23 November 1965, and it was accepted by Pakistan International Airlines, as AP-ATK, on 1 March 1966. In July 1970, Tango Kilo was purchased by the Civil Aviation Administration of China. Later, it was used by the Chinese Air Force, as 50056, and by China United Airlines. (*via GMS*)

Aloha, Hawaiian style! Cowboy and cab wait to greet Hawaiian Airlines passengers arriving at Kamuela in Douglas DC-9-15 N901H. This was the twentieth DC-9 built, and it was accepted by Hawaiian Airlines on 12 March 1966. On 8 December 1971 N901H was bought by Itavia, and it was then sold to Airborne Express in August 1983.
(*via GMS*)

LEFT:
Douglas DC-8-61 N8070U first flew on 14 March 1966 and on 7 May 1967 it was delivered to United Airlines, named *Mainliner Capt R D (Dick) Petty*. In September 1983 N8070U was converted to DC-8-71.

(*via GMS*)

BELOW:
Vickers Super VC-10-1101 G-ARVG at Colombo, Ceylon, photographed on 10 May 1966, is carrying a spare engine in a pod beneath the fuselage centreline. Victor Golf first flew on 17 October 1963 and it was accepted by BOAC on 12 June 1964. In April 1974 G-ARVG was acquired by British Airways when it merged with BOAC. Victor Golf was sold to Gulf Air on 7 October 1975 as A40-VG. In December 1977, after service with Gulf Air, A40-VG was bought by the RAF, and given the serial number ZA141.

(*David Grimer*)

ABOVE:
Boeing 727-46, the 288th 727 built, first flew on 24 June 1966. On 17 July that year it was accepted by Japan Airlines as JA8318 *Tama*. In July 1966 JA8318 was sold to TOA Domestic Airlines, and on 19 March 1972 it was named *Fuji*. In August 1974 Dan-Air bought the aircraft, now G-BDAN, seen here during a trip to Malta. On 25 April 1980 Alpha November crashed into Esperanza Forest, twenty kilometres south of Tenerife Airport.
(*via GMS*)

BELOW:
Douglas DC-8-62 N1501U first flew on 29 August 1966. It was accepted by Scandinavian Airlines System (SAS) as LN-MOO *Sverre Viking* on 20 June 1967. This aircraft crashed into the sea on 13 January 1969, during the approach to Los Angeles, California.
(*via GMS*)

Douglas DC-8-61 N8073U *Mainliner Eric A Johnson* was accepted by United Airlines on 26 January 1967. This aircraft was converted to DC-8-71 configuration in December 1982. (*via GMS*)

This Douglas DC-9-31 was one of
twelve received by Australian airline
Ansett-ANA between 1967 and 1971.
(*via GMS*)

LEFT:
Five Comet Is were lost during the period October 1952 to April 1954 as a result of explosive decompression caused by structural failure in the forward cabins. Once faith was restored, in March 1955 BOAC became the first airline to order second-generation Comet 4s, with a contract for nineteen for use on its African and Far East routes. G-APDB first flew on 27 July 1958. BOAC accepted Delta Bravo on 30 September 1958 and it was one of two Comet 4s which began the first transatlantic jet airliner service. On 2 October 1958 G-APDB made the first transatlantic jet airliner crossing, a press flight to New York, stopping *en route* at Gander. BOAC flew the first London–New York jet service (G-APDC) on 4 October 1958, beating Pan Am's first Boeing 707 transatlantic service by just three weeks. In January 1960 BOAC took delivery of its nineteenth and last Comet 4 (G-APDJ). On 11 September 1965, G-APDB was one of five Comet 4s bought by Malaysian Airways (reregistered 9M-AOB), and it is pictured at Kuching, Sarawak, Malaysia, in 1966. On 30 December 1966 Malaysian Airways became Malaysia-Singapore Airlines. In October 1969 9M-AOB was purchased by Dan Air. With 36,269 flying hours on the airframe, Delta Bravo made its last commercial flight in November 1973. It was delivered to the Imperial War Museum, Duxford on 12 February 1974 where it made its 15,733rd and final landing.
(*Dave Grimer*)

ABOVE:
Air Ceylon Comet 4 G-APDM, photographed in Malaya in the early 1960s. Delta Mike first flew on 21 March 1959 and was accepted by BOAC on 16 April. On 24 March 1967 the aircraft was leased to Middle East Airlines (as OD-AEV), rejoining BOAC on 14 June 1967. On 20 January 1968 G-APDM was leased again, this time to Malaysia-Singapore Airlines, before it rejoined BOAC on 6 January 1969. Dan-Air bought Delta Mike that same month. In May 1974, the aircraft was acquired by the Catering Ground Training Unit at Gatwick, and it is now used for ground training at the airport.
(*Jerry Cullum*)

ABOVE:
Douglas DC-8-61 N822E was accepted by Delta Air Lines on 9 April 1967 as '861'. The aircraft was converted to DC-8-71 in June 1982 and on 9 December 1986 it was bought by United Parcel Service (UPS). N822E was converted again, to DC-8-71F, in July 1988.
(*via GMS*)

BELOW:
Douglas DC-8-63 N1503U flew for the first time on 10 April 1967. It was accepted by KLM Royal Dutch Airlines as PH-DEA *Amerigo Vespucci* on 8 November 1967. In September 1985 Echo Alpha was converted to DC-8-63F for Emery Worldwide Airlines.
(*via GMS*)

Douglas DC-8-62 SE-DBF *Ingvar Viking* was accepted by Scandinavian Airlines System (SAS) on 8 August 1967. On 14 January 1977 Bravo Foxtrot, now N810BN, was bought by Braniff Airways. In February 1986 N810BN was converted to DC-8-62AF. (*via GMS*)

RIGHT:
RIGHT:
Bravo! Bravo! Boeing 727-134 SE-DDB *Northern Light* first flew on 20 November 1967 and it was accepted by Transair Sweden on 2 December. The aircraft transferred to Scanair on 1 October 1969, and it was bought by Philippine Airlines seven days later, now registered RP-C1241. TAME Ecuador bought the aircraft, now HC-BLF, on 19 July 1984
(*GMS*)

BELOW:
A tale of two cities. Douglas DC-9-32 PH-DNG *City of Rotterdam* was accepted by KLM on 21 November 1967. Twenty years later, on 6 March 1987, the Dutch airline sold November Golf to United Aviation Services Inc., and it was renamed *City of Des Moines*.
(*GMS*)

Douglas DC-8-62 HB-IDF *Zurich* was
accepted by Swissair AG on 2 January
1968. In January 1971 HB-IDF
acquired a new name, *Schwyz*, before
being bought by TRATCO in October
1983. After service with Capitol Air,
Nationair bought the aircraft, now
C-GMXY, on 6 August 1985. In 1989
Nationair leased the aircraft to
Zambia Airways and then in June
that year, the airline put X-ray
Yankee out to pasture.
(*via GMS*)

41

Boeing 707-365C G-ATZD *Enterprise* first flew on 29 November 1967, and it was accepted by British Eagle International Airlines on 21 December. Zulu Delta later served with BOAC, British Airways and others, including Libyan Arab and ZAS Airline of Egypt. (*via GMS*)

Wonderful Copenhagen. Douglas DC-9-32 PH-DNK *City of Copenhagen* was accepted on 15 January 1968 by KLM. On 19 August 1988 the Dutch airline sold November Kilo to United Aviation Services Inc. (*GMS*)

ABOVE:
Convair 880-22-1 N830TW of TWA in February 1968. This aircraft had been delivered to TWA seven years earlier, on 25 May 1961. TWA operated N830TW until 1974.
(*Graham Simons*)

BELOW:
A mountain to climb. Douglas DC-8-32 A-ADIM while on lease to SUDFLUG, from 15 March to 31 November 1968. India Mike, then HB-IDA, was accepted by Swissair on 22 April 1960, and it was named *Matterhorn*.
(*Graham Simons*)

OPPOSITE:
Norse pirate. Douglas DC-9-41 N8960U was accepted by Scandinavian Airlines System (SAS) on 23 May 1968 as SE-DBX *Arnljot Viking*.
(*via GMS*)

ABOVE:
Dan-Air stewardesses in front of one of the company's BAC One-Elevens.
(*via GMS*)

45

ABOVE:
Alphabet soup, August 1968. Boeing 727-193 N898PC, which first flew on 17 February 1967, was accepted by Pacific Air Lines on 10 March, and then immediately leased to National. N898PC returned to Pacific on 15 April 1967 and the aircraft was later operated on and off, by Air West and Braniff. Union of Burma Airways bought the aircraft, now XY-ADR, on 9 July 1970, and in October 1976 sold Delta Romeo to Fokker. Dan-Air bought the aircraft, now G-BEGZ, in October 1976. In the 1980s Aravco, a Cayman Islands registered company, bought and operated the aircraft, as VR-CBG and HZ-AMH, before Mike Hotel was sold to Pinecroft as VR-CBG. (*GMS*)

ABOVE:
DC-9-32CF N933F *Calypso Queen*, which was accepted by Overseas National Airways on 14 December 1967. This aircraft was bought by Evergreen International Airlines on 29 October 1976. Airborne Express purchased N933F in July 1981. (*GMS*)

Douglas DC-9-15 XA-SOF *Sonara* of Aeronaves de Mexico (Aeromexico from February 1972), which was accepted on 8 February 1968. It was photographed later that year, in October. Oscar Foxtrot was damaged beyond repair at León, Mexico, on 2 September 1976. In all, 140 DC-9-Series 10s were built for US and overseas airlines, the last being delivered to Aeronaves de Mexico on 27 November 1968.

(*Graham Simons*)

Boeing 707-355C PH-TRF *Prins Bernhard* on lease to Transavia in 1968. This aircraft first flew on 1 November 1967 and it was accepted by Executive Jet Aviation eight days later. Transavia operated Romeo Foxtrot from May to October 1968. The aircraft went on to operate with Caledonian Airways and Monarch, before being bought by Aries World Corporation on 20 July 1984.

48   (*GMS*)

LEFT:
Douglas DC-8-63 N8632 was accepted by Seaboard World Airlines on 16 September 1968. After being leased to several operators, N8632 was converted to DC-8-63CF configuration in April 1984.

BELOW:
Femme fatale. Boeing 727-235 N4740 '40' in October 1968. N4740 first flew on 16 February 1968 and it was accepted by National Airlines on 27 February. In 1971 the aircraft was named *Helen* but was renamed *Ella* in 1975. On 7 January 1980 N4740 became *Clipper Endeavor* in Pan American World Airways' fleet. (*GMS*)

RIGHT:
BAC One-Eleven 409AY TI-1056C *El Tico* of LACSA in October 1968. This aircraft first flew on 6 March 1967 and it was accepted by the Costa Rican airline on 14 April. TACA International Airlines of El Salvador bought *El Tico* on 12 April 1973, and put it into service as YS-01C *El Izalco*. In December 1978 Rolls-Royce/Turbo Union Ltd bought the aircraft and it was registered G-BGTU.
(*GMS*)

BELOW:
BAC One-Eleven 407AW YS-18C *El Salvador* of TACA International Airlines of El Salvador in October 1968. This aircraft first flew on 3 February 1967 and it was accepted on 21 February. Kabo Air bought the aircraft on 11 February 1992 and put it into service as 5N-KBW.
(*GMS*)

Star in the ascendancy. The 737, which appeared in April 1967, has proved another big money-spinner for Boeing, with no fewer than 1,114 Series 200s (which followed the thirty Series 100 models) being delivered by August 1988. Boeing 737-293 N464GB of Air California, pictured in October 1968, first flew on 13 July that year. Air California leased the aircraft on 31 July, and then bought it outright in October 1977. In 1981 N464GB was named *Mariner I*. Appropriately perhaps, Polaris Aircraft Leasing Corporation acquired the aircraft in September 1984.

(*Graham Simons*)

The big one. Texas International
Airlines' Douglas DC-9-15MC N1305T
City of McAllen in November 1968.
N1305T was received by TIA on 22
November 1967. TIA then operated
the aircraft until 31 July 1982, when it
was bought by Air National. Two
years later, on 21 February 1984, the
aircraft was bought by Purolator
Courier Corporation.
(*Graham Simons*)

ABOVE:
Douglas DC-9-32 N3318L '234' of Delta Air Lines in November 1968. This aircraft was accepted by Delta on 10 July 1967, who used it for ten years until February 1977, when it was sold to Ozark Air Lines.
(*Graham Simons*)

BELOW:
Numbers game. Douglas DC-9-15 N93S '903' of Southern Airways in November 1968. This aircraft was accepted by the airline on 28 July 1967. In July 1979 Southern's DC-9s were taken over by Republic Airlines, and '903' became '103'. In October 1986 the aircraft became '9103' in Northwest Airlines' fleet.
(*GMS*)

ABOVE:
Convair 990-30A-5 OB-R-765 of Aerolineas Peruanas SA in December 1968. This aircraft first flew on 30 January 1961 and it was accepted on 8 July 1964 by Garrett Airesearch. It was then leased to Aerolineas Peruanas SA from 1 February 1965 to August 1973.
(*Graham Simons*)

BELOW:
Aloha Hawaii. Douglas DC-9-31 N903H '48' of Hawaiian Airlines in December 1968. This aircraft was accepted on 22 November 1967 and it was operated by Hawaiian Airlines until it was sold to Hughes Airwest on 13 May 1976. The aircraft was later operated by Republic Airlines, as '965', and Northwest Airlines, as '9965'.
(*GMS*)

Boeing 707-355C N525EJ on lease to International Air Bahama, in January 1969. Echo Juliet first flew on 11 May 1967 and was accepted by Executive Jet Aviation (EJA) eight days later. From 20 July 1968 International Air Bahama operated N525EJ and the company returned the aircraft to EJA in October 1969. Echo Juliet was conscripted in November 1989, when it was bought by the USAF.
(*GMS*)

Douglas DC-8-55 PK-GJD *Siliwangi* of Garuda Indonesian Airways at Kai Tak, Hong Kong, in January 1969. Garuda bought the aircraft on 19 July 1966 and it was leased to KLM in March 1969, where it was named *Antony Fokker*. The aircraft returned to Garuda in May 1973 and operated as PK-GEA *Siliwangi* until April 1980, being leased to several companies thereafter.
(*Graham Simons*)

An African Queen. Douglas DC-8-32 N813PA of Air Congo in January 1969. This aircraft was accepted by Pan Am on 13 October 1960 and named *Clipper Bostonian*. Pan Am leased the aircraft to Air Congo on 31 December 1968, and then on 10 June 1969, it was bought outright by Air Congo, as 90-CLE *Kisangani*. After further service with Air Zaire, *Kisangani* was withdrawn from service, and stored at Kinshasa in November 1984. It was broken up in April 1987
(*Graham Simons*)

Douglas DC-8-55F N1509U of Braniff Airways in January 1969. This aircraft was first leased to Pan American-Grace on 2 September 1966, and it was then taken over by Braniff, on 1 February 1967. N1509U was bought by Canadian Pacific Airlines on 17 November 1967 as CF-CPT, and named *Express of Santiago* '608'. It went on to operate with several freight companies, including Flying Tiger Line, CP Air and IAS Cargo Airlines. (*GMS*)

ABOVE:
BAC One-Eleven 215AU of Aloha Airlines, pictured in January 1969, was a titled lady. As *Queen Kaahumanu* this aircraft first flew on 26 May 1967 and it was accepted by the Hawaiian airline on 31 May. Subsequently, *Queen Kaahumanu* was operated by USAir, and Kabo Air.
(*Graham Simons*)

RIGHT:
Ex-American Airlines Convair 990-30A-5 N5617 *Berliner Baer* was bought by Modern Air Transport on 2 February 1968. This aircraft was delivered to American Airlines on 11 May 1962. On 8 May 1975 Modern Air sold the aircraft, now N713NA, to NASA. The aircraft was withdrawn from use and stored at Marana, Arizona, in 1983.

(*via Ben Jones*)

Boeing 727-113C YA-FAR first flew on 22 February 1968 and it was accepted by Ariana Afghan Airlines on 25 March. The following year, on 5 January 1969, Alpha Romeo crashed in fog two kilometres short of the runway at London–Gatwick after descending below the glide slope. Fifty people aboard the aircraft, and two people on the ground, were killed.
(*GMS*)

Halcyon days at Heathrow, on 1 March 1969. The nearest aircraft is BAC One-Eleven G-AWBL *Halcyon Dawn* of Autair International. Behind is a Super One-Eleven of BEA.
(*Graham Dinsdale*)

Saints Go Marching In. Boeing 737-248 EI-ASA *St Jariath* of Aer Lingus first flew on 15 March 1969 and it was accepted by the Irish airline on 28 March.
(*GMS*)

Douglas DC-9-32 N1275L was delivered to Delta Air Lines on 3 April 1969.
(*Graham Simons*)

BOAC Vickers Super VC-10s at London–Heathrow on 17 April 1969.
(*Graham Dinsdale*)

BEA Hawker Siddeley HS 121 Tridents in old and new schemes at London–Heathrow on 17 April 1969. The nearest aircraft is Trident 2E G-AVFK, which first flew on 2 November 1968.
(*Graham Dinsdale*)

BEA Trident 1C G-ARPI at London–Heathrow on 17 April 1969. Papa India first flew on 2 November 1968. It crashed near Staines shortly after take-off from Heathrow on 18 June 1972, killing all 118 passengers and crew.
(*Graham Dinsdale*)

Boeing 707-338C VH-EBT *City of Bendigo* at London–Heathrow's Terminal 3 on 17 April 1969. Bravo Tango first flew on 29 December 1966. The famous 'V jet' logo on the tail is a reference to Australia's involvement in the fan jet engine – the V standing for *Vanus*, the Greek word for fan.
(*Graham Dinsdale*)

BOAC and MEA Boeing 707s and a BOAC Super VC-10 at London–Heathrow on 11 May 1969. A Pan Am DC-8 is on runway 28L. Pan Am was the first airline to order the DC-8, on 11 October 1955, but because the airline had insisted on the longer-ranged Pratt & Whitney JT4A-powered Series 30, it was not until 7 February 1960 that the first aircraft, N803PA, was delivered. In the event Pan Am grew unhappy with the DC-8-30's payload-range performance, and only took delivery of nineteen -31s. All were disposed of by May 1971.
(*Graham Dinsdale*)

China Clipper. Douglas DC-8-32 N8038A '831' of Delta Air Lines in May 1969. This aircraft was first delivered to Pan Am, as N803PA and named *Clipper Mandarin*, on 7 February 1960. Delta bought the aircraft on 30 December 1968, and continued to operate it until January 1974. The aircraft was broken up in October 1984.
(*Graham Simons*)

Caribbean Canuck. Douglas DC-8-61 6Y-JGC of Air Jamaica in May 1969. Air Jamaica bought Golf Charlie from original owners, Air Canada, on 25 March 1969. The Canadian airline had accepted CF-TJX '864' on 29 April 1968, and on 22 October 1973 bought it back from Air Jamaica. The aircraft was later leased to several carriers, and in January 1988 it was converted to DC-8-61F.

(*GMS*)

BAC One-Eleven 402AP PI-C1151 of TAE in May 1969. This aircraft first flew on 20 September 1968. It was bought by Spanish carrier Trabajos Aereos y Enclaces SA, being accepted on 1 March 1969 as EC-BQF. BAC repossessed the aircraft in February 1970, and it was registered G-AYHM. After a spell on lease to Bavaria Fluggesellschaft, on 11 August 1972 Hotel Mike, now YR-BCH, was bought by TAROM. TAROM had begun its Bucharest to London–Gatwick BAC One-Eleven service on 22 June 1968. (*GMS*)

ABOVE:
Highland Fling. Dramatic take-off shot of Boeing 707-399C G-AVTW *County of Ayr* in May 1969. Tango Whiskey first flew on 15 December 1967 and it was accepted by Caledonian Airways on 29 December. Tango Whiskey later flew with TAP in the 1970s, and Nigeria Airways and Dominicana in the 1980s, before it was finally withdrawn from use and stored at Santo Domingo in the Dominican Republic.
(*Stan Lee*)

BELOW:
The eagle has landed. BAC One-Eleven 304AX CF-QBO *La Royaume du Château Sanguency* of Quebecair in August 1969. This aircraft first flew on 12 May 1967 and on 25 May 1967 it was accepted by British Eagle International Airlines as G-ATPI and named *Supreme*. Quebecair sold the aircraft to Airways International Cymru in November 1984.
(*GMS*)

Aviogenex Tupolev Tu-134 YU-AHI at Ringway Airport, Manchester, in September 1969. Tu-134s were first delivered to the Yugoslavian airline in January 1969.

(*via Barry Reeve*)

Queen of the skies. Deliveries of twenty-five Boeing 747-121s to Pan Am started on 12 December 1969. The airline flew over 300 employees from New York to London on 12 January 1970. N735PA *Clipper Young America*, which had been delivered just three days earlier, landed at London–Heathrow, three hours late after one of its Pratt & Whitney JT9D fan-jet engines had problems and had to be changed. On 21 January 1970 Pan Am began a scheduled Boeing 747 commercial service with non-stop flights between New York and London, when N736PA *Clipper Victor* completed the flight after N733PA *Clipper Constitution* had suffered engine problems at JFK Airport. (*Walt Truax*)

ABOVE:
Boeing 727-86 EP-IRA *Isfahan* of Iran Air in December 1969. EP-IRA first flew on 25 June 1966 and was used by Iran Air until 7 January 1983, when it was destroyed while taxiing at Tehran Airport, Iran.
(*Graham Simons*)

BELOW:
When in Rome. Douglas DC-9-33RC PH-DNZ *City of Rome* was accepted by KLM on 6 February 1970. November Zulu was bought back by Douglas, and after a period on lease to VIASA was acquired by the US Navy on 27 June 1983.
(*Ron Green*)

The last word in comfort, sixties style, onboard an Eastern Airlines Boeing 727.
(*via GMS*)

Douglas DC-9-15RC N8908 of Continental Airlines in February 1970. This aircraft was accepted by Continental on 22 September 1967 and operated by the airline until 1 May 1973, when N8908 was sold to Air Canada as CF-TOU. On 5 February 1981 Air Florida bought the aircraft, now N65AF.

(*Graham Simons*)

Banana-yellow Douglas DC-8-62 N1803 of Braniff Airways in April 1970. Braniff, whose liveries rivalled a packet of Opal Fruits, accepted this aircraft on 22 August 1967. In January 1970 it was leased to Pan Am, where it was named *Clipper Golden Light*, until 31 March 1971. International Air Leases bought the aircraft in November 1983 and it was leased to Hawaiian Airlines before conversion, in July 1985, to DC-8-62F.

(*GMS*)

Boeing 707-309C B-1824 of China Airlines in April 1970. This aircraft first flew on 27 October 1969 and it was accepted by China Airlines on 7 November. In September 1982, B-1824 was sold to Ansalt-Anret SA, and later, as N707ZS, *Maritza*, it was used as a freighter for Jet Cargo Inc. (*GMS*)

Dutch treat. Douglas DC-8-63 PH-DEM *James Cook* of KLM at Schiphol Airport, Amsterdam, in the early 1970s. Echo Mike was accepted by the Dutch airline on 22 June 1970, and it was operated in Holland for five years. On 3 November 1975 it was leased to Surinam Airways, who named it *25 November*. Echo Mike returned to KLM in October 1983, and it was then leased to African Safari Airways. (*GMS*)

French leave. Boeing 727-228 F-BOJC and 727-224 5A-DAI at London–Heathrow in the early 1970s. Juliet Charlie first flew on 19 April 1968 and it was accepted by Air France on 2 May that year. 5A-DAI first flew on 13 June 1969 and it was delivered to Libyan Arab Airlines on 22 January 1971, after first being allocated to Continental Airlines. (*CONAM*)

British European Airways (BEA) Hawker Siddeley Aviation HS 121-3B Trident G-AWZD taxiing in at London–Heathrow in the early 1970s. Zulu Delta first flew on 5 March 1971 and it was accepted by BEA on 26 March 1971. From 1974 G-AWZD served with British Airways before it was bought by Air Charter Service, on 24 July 1985.
(*CONAM*)

ABOVE:
Boeing 737-230QC D-ABFE *Trier* at Prestwick in 1970. This aircraft first flew on 4 February 1970 and it was accepted by Lufthansa on 11 February. Lufthansa operated Foxtrot Echo until September 1985.

(*Dave Grimer*)

BELOW:
Convair 990 OD-AFJ of Middle East Airlines in July 1970. Foxtrot Juliet was accepted by American Airlines as N5601 on 18 January 1963. American Airlines received its first Convair 990 on 8 January 1962 and the airline began an inaugural service on 18

March. From 1965 American Airlines began disposing of its 990A fleet as more fuel-efficient aircraft became available, and N5601 was bought by MEA on 19 September 1969. After ending its airline service, Foxtrot Juliet was broken up in March 1981.

(*Graham Simons*)

Boeing 707-321 YU-AGA in August 1970 while on lease to Jugoslovenski Aerotransport (from 24 May 1970 to July 1974). Golf Alpha first flew on 21 October 1959. It was accepted by Pan Am as N723PA and named *Clipper Viking*.
(*GMS*)

BAC Super One-Eleven 501EX
G-AWYU, pictured at Gatwick in 1970,
first flew on 10 June 1969. Yankee
Uniform was delivered to British
United Airways (BUA), seven days
later. British Caledonian Airways
merged with BUA on 30 November
1970, and in 1971 G-AWYU was
named *Isle of Colonsay*. The aircraft
was renamed *County of Avon*, after the
merger to form British Airways, on 14
April 1988.
(*Tony Hudson*)

Saintly Norse god. Boeing 720-048 EI-
ALA (LN-TUU) *Roald Amundsen* of
Trans Polar in February 1971. Lima
Alpha first flew on 14 October 1960. It
was accepted by Aer Lingus on 25
October, and named *St Patrick*. Trans
Polar bought the aircraft on 16 October
1970, but it was repossessed by Aer
Lingus on 18 May 1971 and renamed
St Pappin. Lima Alpha was operated
later by Club International Inc.,
Pioneer International (as *City of
Niagara Falls*), Hanna Industries and
finally, Aero-america, before being
scrapped in 1983.
(*GMS*)

American amigo. Douglas DC-8-55F EC-BMV *Pedro Berruguette* was accepted by Iberia on 31 March 1968. The Spanish airline retired Mike Victor from its fleet in December 1984. Douglas DC-9-32 EC-BYH *Ciuda de Cadiz* was accepted by Iberia on 10 April 1972, and in April 1980 Yankee Hotel was leased to Aviaco. EC-BYH was damaged beyond economical repair while landing at Granada, Spain, on 30 March 1992. (*CONAM*)

Douglas DC-8-53 PH-DCM of VIASA in the early 1970s. Charlie Mike was accepted by KLM on 24 June 1961 and named *Henry Dunant*, operating in joint KLM/VIASA livery until October 1970. On 15 July 1974 *Henry Dunant* was leased to Venezuelan airline VIASA, now registered VY-C-VIG, and later, YV-129C. On 9 March 1984, it was withdrawn from service and bought by International Air Leases, before being broken up at Opa Locka, Florida, in May 1985.
(*GMS*)

ABOVE:
Douglas DC-9-32 OE-LDF *Salzburg* of Austrian Airlines, which was accepted on 2 December 1971. Behind is Boeing 727-2H3 TS-JHV *Jugurtha* of Tunis Air, which first flew on 31 May 1977, and was accepted on 10 June that year.
(*Ron Green*)

LEFT:
Douglas DC-8-52 ZK-NZA of Air New Zealand in February 1972. Zulu Alpha was accepted by Air New Zealand on 19 July 1965, and it was leased to KLM as PH-ADA in 1969. The aircraft returned to Air New Zealand on 20 September 1969 and was used until 24 January 1977, when it was bought by Evergreen International Airlines. The aircraft was finally broken up in February 1984.
(*GMS*)

ABOVE:
Boeing 707-331C N5773T of Golden Sun Air Cargo in June 1972. This aircraft first flew on 16 September 1967 and it was accepted on 29 September by TWA, who leased it to Golden Sun from 14 December 1971 to 25 March 1972.
(*Graham Simons*)

RIGHT:
Transavia Holland Boeing 707-123B PH-TVA *Provincie Zeeland* in Spain in 1972. This aircraft first flew on 12 July 1959 and it was accepted on 24 August by American Airlines as N7519A *Flagship Kentucky*. Transavia acquired the aircraft on 17 March 1972. Guy America Airways bought PH-TVA, now N519GA, on 8 April 1982. Boeing bought the 707 back in April 1983 and it was used for parts in the KC-135E programme before it was finally broken up.

(*Mike Bailey*)

Flying Finn. Jugoslovenski Aero-transport Douglas DC-9-32 YU-UHU and Finnair Caravelle S.E.212.10B3 OH-LSH *Kuopio*, at London–Heathrow in the early 1970s. Hotel Uniform was delivered to Jugoslovenski Aero-transport on 7 May 1971. Finnair operated fifteen Sud-Aviation Caravelles at various times, OH-LSH flying for the first time on 13 January 1967 and being delivered to Finnair on 20 January. In December 1981, Sierra Hotel was bought by Europe Aero Service, who retired *Kuopio* in August 1991.

(*CONAM*)

RIGHT:
Douglas DC-9-15 N968E of Ozark Air
Lines at Orange County Airport,
California, in the early 1970s. This
aircraft was accepted by Swissair on
10 March 1967, registered HB-IFD and
named *Glarus*. Douglas bought the
aircraft in August 1968, and on 8 July
1969 leased the aircraft, now HP-505
and named *Marco Tulio Hooper*, to Air
Panama. On 22 November 1972 the
aircraft (now N1791U) returned to
Douglas, and Ozark became
its next owner, when the airline
purchased the aircraft on 7 December
1972. Ozark operated N968E for two
years, selling the aircraft on 28 March
1974 to Texas International Airlines,
who named it *City of Little Rock*.
Continental Airlines took over the
aircraft on 31 October 1982.
(*GMS*)

BELOW:
Indian summer. BAC One-Eleven
203AE N1134J of Mohawk Airlines,
Utica, New York, in February 1973.
This aircraft first flew on 3 November
1965 and it was accepted by Braniff
Airways five days later. Mohawk
bought the aircraft in September 1970
and it was later operated by Allegheny
Airlines and USAir.
(*GMS*)

Boeing 707-370C YI-AGE first flew on 14 August 1974 and it was delivered to Iraqi Airways on 27 August. Golf Echo was leased to Arab Air Cargo from April 1982 to December 1985, at the end of which Iraqi Airways retired the aircraft.

(*Graham Simons*)

Connecticut Yankee. Boeing 720-023B N7528A *Flagship Connecticut* of American Airlines. This aircraft was built as an -023 and it first flew on 24 June 1960. N7528A was accepted by American Airlines on 24 July, being converted to 720-023B in September 1961. On 10 May 1974 this aircraft, now G-BCBA, was leased to Invicta Airlines. After retirement by American Airlines in October 1974, this aircraft was operated by several carriers, including Tempair International, Monarch, Cyprus Airways and Royal Air Maroc, before being bought by Boeing in January 1986 to be used in the KC-135E programme. The aircraft was finally broken up for spares at Tucson, Arizona, in June 1991.

(*GMS*)

LEFT:
Bonnie Scot. Vickers VC-10-1103 7Q-YKH was bought by Air Malawi on 25 November 1974. This aircraft first flew on 30 September 1964 as G-ASIW, and it was accepted by British United Airways on the same day. When BUA merged with Caledonian, India Whiskey was christened *Loch Lomond*. Air Malawi operated the VC-10 until 1979. It was scrapped in 1981.
(*Tony Hudson*)

BELOW:
Boeing 737-2H6 9M-ASR of Malaysian Airline System in January 1975. Sierra Romeo first flew on 28 August 1974 and it was accepted on 9 September that year. In December 1975 the aircraft was reregistered 9M-MBH.
(*GMS*)

Boeing 737-2A6 VR-BEH of Maritime Investment and Shipping Co. Ltd in January 1975. This aircraft first flew on 31 July 1969 as N520L and it was accepted by LTV Corporation on 25 August. Maritime Investment and Shipping Co. Ltd bought the aircraft on 27 April 1972, and operated it until 10 October 1980, when it was sold to the John W. Mecom Co. (*GMS*)

Roving Kiwi. Boeing 737-22 ZK-NAM of New Zealand National Airways Corporation in March 1975. (National merged with Air New Zealand on 1 April 1978.) This aircraft first flew on 9 March 1968 as N737W (from 1 July 1970, N1359B) and it was accepted by National on 15 February 1974. International Lease Finance Corporation bought the aircraft, now ZK-NAM, on 18 April 1986 and leased it, first to Frontier Airlines and then to Continental.
(*GMS*)

Pacific performer. BAC One-Eleven 479FU DQ-FBV of Fijian airline Air Pacific in March 1975. This aircraft first flew on 16 July 1973 and it was accepted by Air Pacific on 4 August. In March 1984 DQ-FBV was bought by the Empire Test Pilots' School. (*GMS*)

Boeing 737-248 EI-ASB *St Albert* of Aer Lingus in July 1975. Sierra Bravo first flew on 2 April 1969 and it was accepted by the Irish airline on 15 April. Compania Inter-America Export-Import bought *St Albert* on 31 March 1987, and after leasing it to Aer Lingus in early 1987, leased it as OB-R-1314 to Peruvian airline, Faucett, named *Juana de Arco*. The aircraft was damaged beyond repair while landing at Iquitos, Peru, on 3 April 1989. (*GMS*)

DETA Mozambique Airlines Boeing 737-2B1 CR-BAA in October 1975. This aircraft first flew on 4 December 1969 and it was delivered to DETA six days later.
(*Graham Simons*)

Boeing 737-2J8C ST-AFL of Sudan
Airways in October 1975. Foxtrot Lima
first flew on 11 September that year,
and it was delivered seven days later.
(*GMS*)

South American samba. Aero Peru Douglas DC-8-53 OB-R1083 in December 1975. Aero Peru bought the aircraft from VIASA on 15 July 1974, then sold it back to Douglas on 7 July 1976. R1083 was converted to DC-8-54F in March 1977 and went on to operate with Transmeridian Air Cargo, as *Lady Jane*, and LAC Colombia, as HK-2632X and renamed *Mary De Donado*.
(*GMS*)

Douglas DC-8-63PF F-BOLL of Union de Transports Aériens (UTA) in December 1975. This aircraft was accepted by Eastern Airlines on 21 November 1969, and it was then bought by UTA on 30 April 1973. F-BOLL was destroyed by a bomb at Ndjamena, Chad, on 10 March 1984.
(*GMS*)

Viking saga. Douglas DC-8-63 HS-TGZ *Srianocha* of Thai Airways International in December 1975. This aircraft was accepted as SE-DBH *Ring Viking* on 18 September 1968 by SAS, who leased it to Thai Airways on 27 March 1974. On 1 November that year, Thai Airways bought the aircraft outright. After many years' service with several operators on lease, HS-TGZ was repurchased by SAS on 1 April 1986. Now SE-DBH and named *Dana Viking*, the aircraft was operated by Scanair. The aircraft was converted to DC-8-63F in April 1989. Aer Turas bought the aircraft, now EI-CGO, on 25 April. (*GMS*)

BELOW:
Boeing 737-281 JA8401 of All Nippon Airways in March 1976. This aircraft first flew on 12 May 1969 and was delivered to ANA on 22 May. Boeing bought the airliner back on 14 April 1976, selling it to China Airlines as B-1870. On 16 February 1986, B-1870 crashed into the sea six kilometres from Makung, Taiwan, after an aborted landing.
(*Graham Simons*)

LEFT:
Sud-Aviation S.E.210-11R Caravelle EC-BRX *Renacuajo* of Trans Europa at Norwich Airport in May 1976. This aircraft first flew on 21 July 1969 and it was delivered to Iberia nine days later. Romeo X-ray was bought by Trans Europa in 1973, who operated *Renacuajo* until August 1982, at which time it was bought by Aerosucre Colombia as HK-2850X. On 27 November 1986 it was damaged beyond economical repair after overrunning the runway at Arauca.
(*Ron Green*)

Scottish visitor. BAC One-Eleven 510-ED G-AVMJ *Strathclyde Region* at London–Heathrow in June 1976. Mike Juliet first flew on 15 July 1968, and it was delivered to BEA on 29 August 1969. G-AVMJ was withdrawn from service, and in January 1992 it was stored at Bournemouth–Hurn.
(*Ron Green*)

Air France Sud-Aviation S.E.210 Caravelle F-BHRV *Provence* at London–Heathrow in June 1976. Romeo Victor first flew on 15 November 1960 and it was accepted by Air France on 22 November that year. F-BHRV was withdrawn from use in December 1980 and scrapped.
(*Ron Green*)

Tupolev Tu-134 LZ-TUB of Bulgarian
Balkan Airlines, one of eleven Tu-134s
ordered by the airline in 1970. LZ-TUB
is shown at London–Heathrow in June
1976.

(*Ron Green*)

Double century. Douglas DC-8-32 N1776R of Overseas National Airways in a colourful American bicentennial colour scheme in 1976. This aircraft was accepted by Northwest Orient Airlines as N801US on 18 May 1960. Overseas bought the aircraft on 20 September 1974 and leased it to several airlines before it returned to ONA in June 1980. It was broken up at Jedda, Saudi Arabia, in March 1981.

(*Graham Simons*)

Dan-Air Comet 4Bs at Manchester in March 1978. The famous 'black sheds' have since gone to make way for the airport's second runway. G-APZM first flew on 30 June 1960 and it was accepted by BEA on 14 July. BEA leased Zulu Mike to Olympic, who named the Comet *Queen Sophia*. Channel Airways bought G-APZM on 14 May 1970, and Dan-Air acquired it on 17 April 1972. Dan-Air became the largest and last commercial operator of the Comet, using no fewer than forty-eight 4s, 4Bs and 4Cs between 1966 and 1975. G-APZM was broken up in September 1980.
(*Graham Dinsdale*)

Boeing 727-222 N72601U flew for the first time on 4 April 1978 and it was accepted by United Airlines on 12 April.
(*United Airlines*)

Burning the midnight oil. Dan-Air
Boeing 727 at London–Gatwick at
23.00 hours on 11 May 1979.
(*Graham Simons*)

Double scotch at Schiphol. Fokker F28-4000 Fellowship G-JCWW first flew on 10 October 1978 as PH-EXR. Air Anglia bought the aircraft on 21 May 1979, and it became G-JCWW on 3 June. (WW for 'Wilbur' Wright, one of the founders and directors. Sister ship, G-WWJC was for Jim Crampten.)

Whiskey Whiskey became F-GDFD when Air Alsace acquired the aircraft on 1 May 1981 after leasing it the previous year. On 15 March 1996 the famous name of Fokker disappeared when the seventy-seven-year-old Dutch company announced bankruptcy. (*via CONAM*)

Island hopping. Air UK BAC One-Eleven 432FD G-AXOX *Island Endeavour* at London–Gatwick in the early 1980s. Oscar X-ray first flew on 28 August 1968 and it was accepted by Bahamas Airways on 11 November.

After serving with Gulf Air, in June 1978 G-AXOX was bought by British Island Airways, and it was later leased by Air UK. (*via CONAM*)

Boeing 707-384C SX-DBC *City of Knossos* pictured in the early 1980s at London–Heathrow. This aircraft first flew on 14 June 1966 and it was accepted by Olympic Airways four days later. Israeli Aircraft Industries bought the aircraft on 6 March 1990, and in January 1991 it was acquired by the Venezuelan Air Force.
(*Ron Green*)

Boeing 707-365C G-ATZD of BOAC at London–Heathrow in the early 1970s. Zulu Delta first flew on 29 November 1967 and it was accepted by British Eagle as *Enterprise* on 21 December. After operating on lease to Middle East Airlines, from 1 March to October 1968, G-ATZD was purchased by BOAC on 6 December that year. British Airways sold G-ATZD to TRATCO in May 1983. Zulu Delta was to see widespread operation with several European and Middle Eastern cargo airlines, including Alia-Royal Jordanian Airlines.

(*CONAM*)

Greek tragedy. Boeing 727-2H9s YU-AKA and YU-AKI of Jugoslovenski Aerotransport at London–Heathrow in the early 1970s. Kilo Alpha first flew on 31 May 1974 and it was accepted on 7 June. Kilo India first flew on 23 October 1980 and was delivered to Jugoslovenski Aerotransport on 15 December 1980. On 1 May 1987 YU-AKA, now TC-AKD, was leased to Talia Airways. During a flight to Cyprus on 27 February 1988, it struck a mountain during its approach and crashed at Arapkoy.

(*Ron Green*)

Boeing 707-386C EP-IRL *Apadana* of Iran Air flanked by BOAC Super VC-10-1101 G-ARVH and a passing Olympic Airways 707. Romeo Lima first flew on 15 December 1969 and it was accepted by Iran Air on the last day of 1969. Victor Hotel first flew on 22 November 1963 and it was delivered to BOAC on 2 July 1964. *(CONAM)*

Romeo, Romeo ... Douglas DC-8-43 I-DIWR *Nicoloso da Recco* of Alitalia taxiing out at London–Heathrow in the early 1970s. Whiskey Romeo was first delivered to Alitalia on 1 February 1962 and it was leased to Zambia Airways from June 1969 to early summer 1971. This roving romeo had many other owners, and it was converted to DC-8-54F in November 1978.
(*CONAM*)

Boeing 707-430 G-APFP (foreground), first flew on 29 November 1960, and it was delivered to BOAC on 22 December 1960. Boeing bought Foxtrot Papa in October 1975, and in January 1976 the company donated it to the Franklin Institute in Philadelphia, where it was put on display. (*CONAM*)

Zulu warriors. BEA Tridents at London–Heathrow in the early 1970s. Trident 1C G-ARPX first flew on 13 May 1966 and it was delivered to BEA on 25 May 1966. Trident 3B G-AWZO first flew on 9 February 1972 and was accepted by BEA on 16 February. Zulu Oscar was donated to Hatfield on 18 April 1986 for use as a ground trainer. (*CONAM*)

Douglas DC-9-32 PK-GNJ *Woyla* was delivered to Garuda Indonesian Airways on 26 June 1975. In July 1982, now D-ALLC, it was bought by Aero Lloyd.
(*Graham Simons*)

A rose by any other name. Boeing 727-233 C-GAAC '403' of Air Canada in July 1975, This aircraft first flew on 2 October 1974 and it was accepted by Air Canada seven days later. Alpha Charlie was bought by Federal Express on 31 March 1985 and named *Emily Rose*. In August 1985 the Boeing 727-233 was converted to -233F Freighter configuration. (*GMS*)

RIGHT:
Sud-Aviation S.E.210B3 YK-AFD of Syrianair at Athens in the late 1970s. This aircraft first flew on 5 April 1966 and it was accepted by Sterling Airways as OY-STB three days later. Syrian Arab Airlines bought OY-STB in November 1971. Syrian Arab Airlines became Syrianair in 1977.

(*Tony Hudson*)

Dan-Air BAC Super One-Eleven 518FG G-BDAT at Ringway Airport, Manchester, in July 1977. Alpha Tango first flew on 29 January 1971 and it was accepted by Court Line as *Halcyon Dawn* on 18 March. After operating with British Caledonian from August 1974, Alpha Tango was bought by Dan-Air on 31 January 1975. (*via Barry Reeve*)

Boeing 707-3F9C SN-ANO *Obudu Hills* first flew on 10 December 1977 and it was delivered to Nigeria Airways on 30 January 1978.
(*Ron Green*)

A town like Alice or a Tasmanian Devil? QANTAS Boeing 707-338C VH-EAG *Alice Springs* on 26 March 1979, at the end of its last flight with the airline, from Melbourne to Sydney. It was sold to the RAAF to become A20-627 *Windsor Town*. Alpha Golf first flew on 30 April 1968 and it was accepted by QANTAS on 16 May 1968 as *City of Hobart*.
(*Author's Coll*)

LEFT:
Tattooed lady. Boeing 720-023BF HC-BDP of Ecuatoriana at Los Angeles in the late 1970s. This aircraft first flew on 27 April 1961 and it was accepted by American Airlines on 23 May. Operated by Pan Am as *Clipper Carib* until July 1974, Ecuatoriana purchased it in April 1977. HC-BDP was scrapped in the late 1980s, after being used by Boeing in its KC-135E programme.
(*Tony Hudson*)

Index